For Raziyah the Great!

Travel With Me From A to Z!

Written By: RENATA "NyceWitIt" SMITH
Illustrated By: RAZIYAH A. SMITH

Hello,
My name is Raziyah. Would you like to travel the world with me today? Fantastic, this is going to be exciting!

The first place I would like to visit is **Australia**, to view the koala bears. Did you know that koala bears are only pregnant for 35 days before giving birth? When the baby koala is born, it is blind, bald, and earless. Koala bears love to sleep, napping up to 20 hours a day after getting comfy on their favorite branch of the tree. They have five fingers just like you and me.

Brazil has Jaguars, which are really large cats. They can be over six feet long. Can you imagine that?

Columbia is a great place to learn how to salsa dance, but it takes practice you won't learn from just a glance!

The Democratic Republic of the Congo is the only country with the Okapi, an animal mixed with a giraffe and zebra. The unique patterns are such a sight to see.

Egypt is the home of the Pyramids, built back in the B.C days. Walking through the halls is like going through a maze.

France is famous for the Eiffel Tower located in the city of Paris. The structure has 1,665 stairs to the top. How many could you climb before having to stop?

Let's head to **Greece** to see the dolphins, four out of the thirty-six types live here. Striped dolphin, Risso's dolphin, Common dolphin, and Bottlenose dolphin. I love to see them jump through the sky. It's like a giant fish that can also fly.

Honduras has an island called Utila. This island is known as one of the world's best places for viewing whale sharks. The whale shark only swims three mph and measures twelve meters long. Snorkelers love to visit the waters to see them swim along.

Italy, I am soooooooo happy that we are here because it means that pizza is near! Yummy! Pizza was invented in Naples, Italy, in the 18th century, when the city's poor people got creative and began adding tomatoes to their yeast-based flat bread after discovering that tomatoes were not poisonous as Europeans once believed. Pizza is my most favorite dish of all, so I am quite relieved.

Japan still has an active volcano called Mount Fuji. It is the tallest volcano in Japan. The first eruption happened before I was born. In December of 1707, is when it all began.

Kenya has excellent safaris, and while we are on tour, we will see lions, elephants, buffalos, rhinos, leopards, and more.

Las Vegas, Nevada, USA, has an Indian Village called Supai located inside the Grand Canyon. It is considered the most remote and isolated community in the United States, which means the community is separated from others. Supai only has a population of about 208 people. All supplies provided to the village are brought in by helicopters and animals, mostly mules, pretty old fashion but saves fuel.

Mexico created a holiday called "The Day of the Dead," which is celebrated from October 31st - November 2nd. This holiday is a loving time that helps people remember the deceased and honor their memory with food, drinks, costumes, face painting, and parades. Flowers are brought to gravesites, and families pray.

Namibia is the cheetah capital of the world! Adult cheetahs can weigh between 75 to 125 pounds and reach up to 7.5 feet in length. Cheetahs are flexible and fast, reaching speeds of 70 mph. They hunt gazelles, impalas, rodents, hares, and birds. Unlike goats, sheep, and llamas, they do not travel in herds.

Thousands of sea turtles migrate every year to the shores of **Oman** to lay 50,000 to 60,000 eggs. After about two months, the eggs hatch, and the baby turtles move into the sea. But nothing is more astonishing about Oman than the vast number of beautiful castles, some of which are the Jibreen Castle, Al Hazm Castle, and the Ras al Hadd Castle, and they allow tours for those willing to travel.

Portugal is surrounded by mountains and beaches, making it great for several different activities like gathering seashells along the coast, boat tours that take you into the sea caves, and even watching some surfers ride the waves.

Qatar has one of the most uniquely designed museums ever made. **The Museum of Islamic Art.** The five-story building is located on a man-made island sixty meters from the shore of Doha's Corniche. The building is connected to the coast by three bridges. The museum displays art from the 7th century to the 19th century and even has its own library, prayer rooms, a playground, and a café. There is a very strict dress code required to honor the Qatari culture. Don't leave before viewing the outside 78-foot-high sculpture.

Russia is the largest country in the world. This country has an estimated brown bear population of around 100,000, which is why the bear is one of the most familiar images associated with Russia. Brown bears can weigh between 220lbs to 780lbs. I don't want to be near when one comes around!

Gender-specific tattooing is a part of Samoan culture. Tattoos for men are called **Pe'a** and are made up of geometrical patterns that are tribe and tradition-specific. The tattoo covers from the knees up to the ribs. A woman is given a **Malu**, which covers the area from just below her knees to her upper thighs. These tattoos represent the spiritual and cultural heritage of Samoa. Getting a tattoo in **Samoa** is a painful process. They are done with traditional tools made from bone, tusk, shark teeth, shells, and wood. This process begins while still in childhood.

Turkey is known for the creation of the Shish Kebab. Turkish soldiers used their swords to grill marinated meat over an open fire during the war. Today Turkish kebabs are made of lamb, beef, or chicken slowly roasted on a stick and are usually served with fresh vegetables, pita, and garlicky yogurt sauce. What a delicious meal to come across.

Arabian oryx is an antelope you can find in the **United Arab Emirates**. These animals live in desert-like areas and eat healthy diets consisting of plants, wild melons, and roots they dig out of the ground. Arabian oryx are not fast animals but have incredible stamina capable of walking up to 43 miles in just one night, making it to a new city by daylight.

Angel Falls is the world's highest uninterrupted waterfall. It is located in **Venezuela**. The waterfall drops over the Auyán-tepui mountain located in the Canaima National Park, a park that is almost the size of Belgium. The waterfall is surrounded by wildlife consisting of monkeys, poison-arrow frogs, snakes, 500 species of orchids, monkeys, and many others. Visitors come to the park to visit the jungles, mountain climb, and skydive off the Falls. This kind of bravery deserves a round of applause.

The White House is the home of the President of the United States and his family. It is also a museum of American history, located in **Washington DC.**, the capital of the United States of America. The White House has 6 levels consisting of 132 rooms, 35 bathrooms, 412 doors, 147 windows, 28 fireplaces, 8 staircases, and 3 elevators. It took eight years to complete and cost $232,372 to build. It is highly guarded by members of the secret service who must remain alert and highly skilled.

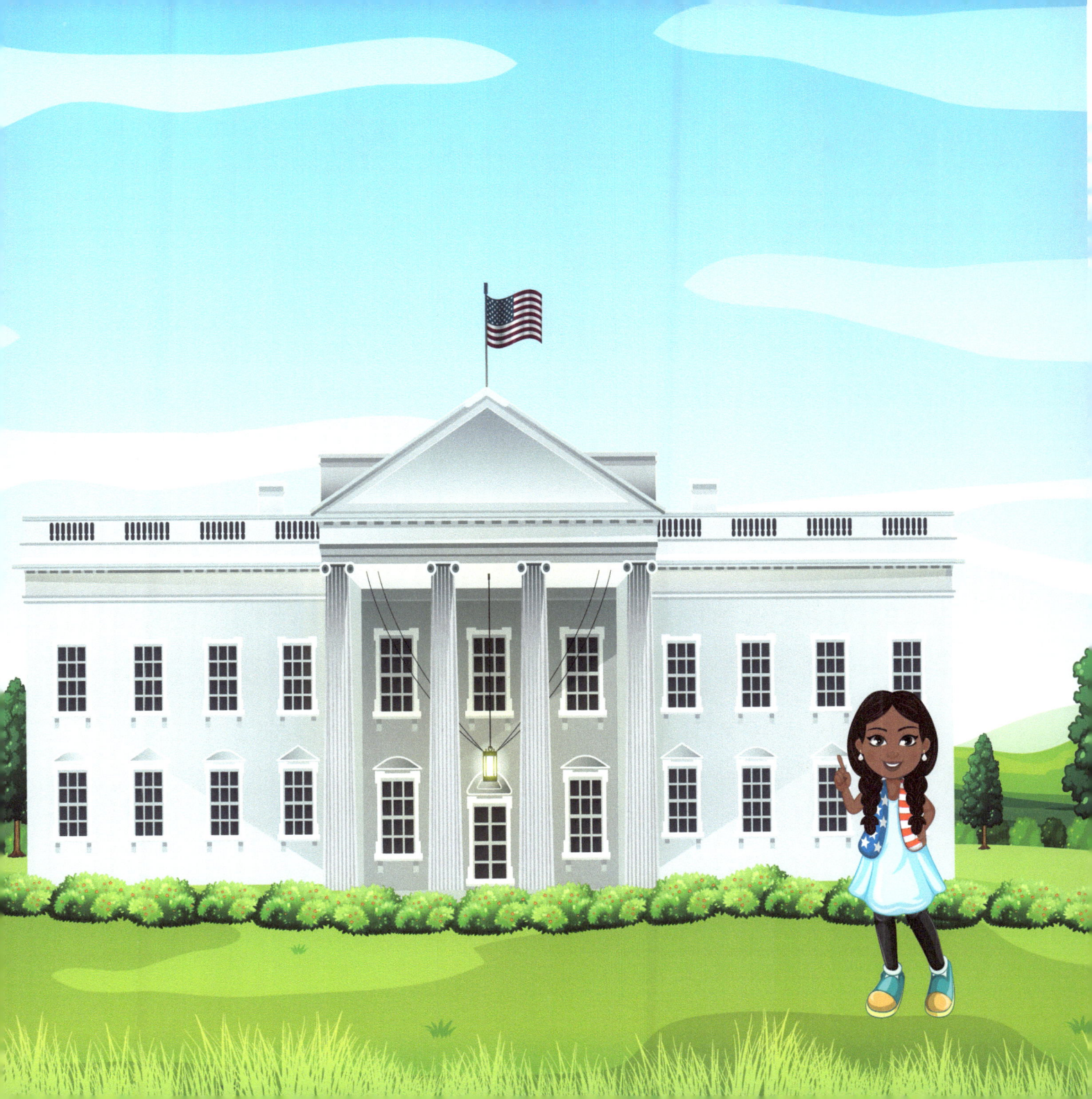

Tang Paradise is the first Tang Dynasty royal garden-style large-scale theme park in **Xi'an, China,** that holds the record of having the world's largest water show. Programs include drum and stilt performances, magic acrobatics, stage plays, and even dance and opera shows. These events are far more exciting than staying at home playing tic-tac-toe. Come on, let's go!!!

Yemen has trees called "The Dragon Blood Tree," which resembles an umbrella. The tree grows in a mushroom shape, with thick branches and leaves on the ends that form in clusters. This tree produces red sap, so when it is cut, it gives the appearance that the tree is bleeding. Almost like a human being, strange but makes for good sightseeing.

Zimbabwe has a small tribe called the Vadoma People, also referred to as the "two-toed tribe" or "ostrich people." Some were born with a genetic deficiency known as lobster claw syndrome. This medical condition causes a defect resulting in the absence of the three middle toes, and the remaining toes curl inward. One in every four children in the family inherits this defect. Tribal law forbids members to marry outside of the group, so this abnormality stays within the tribe.

Well, That's the end of our travel. Thanks for coming along for the ride! See you next time!

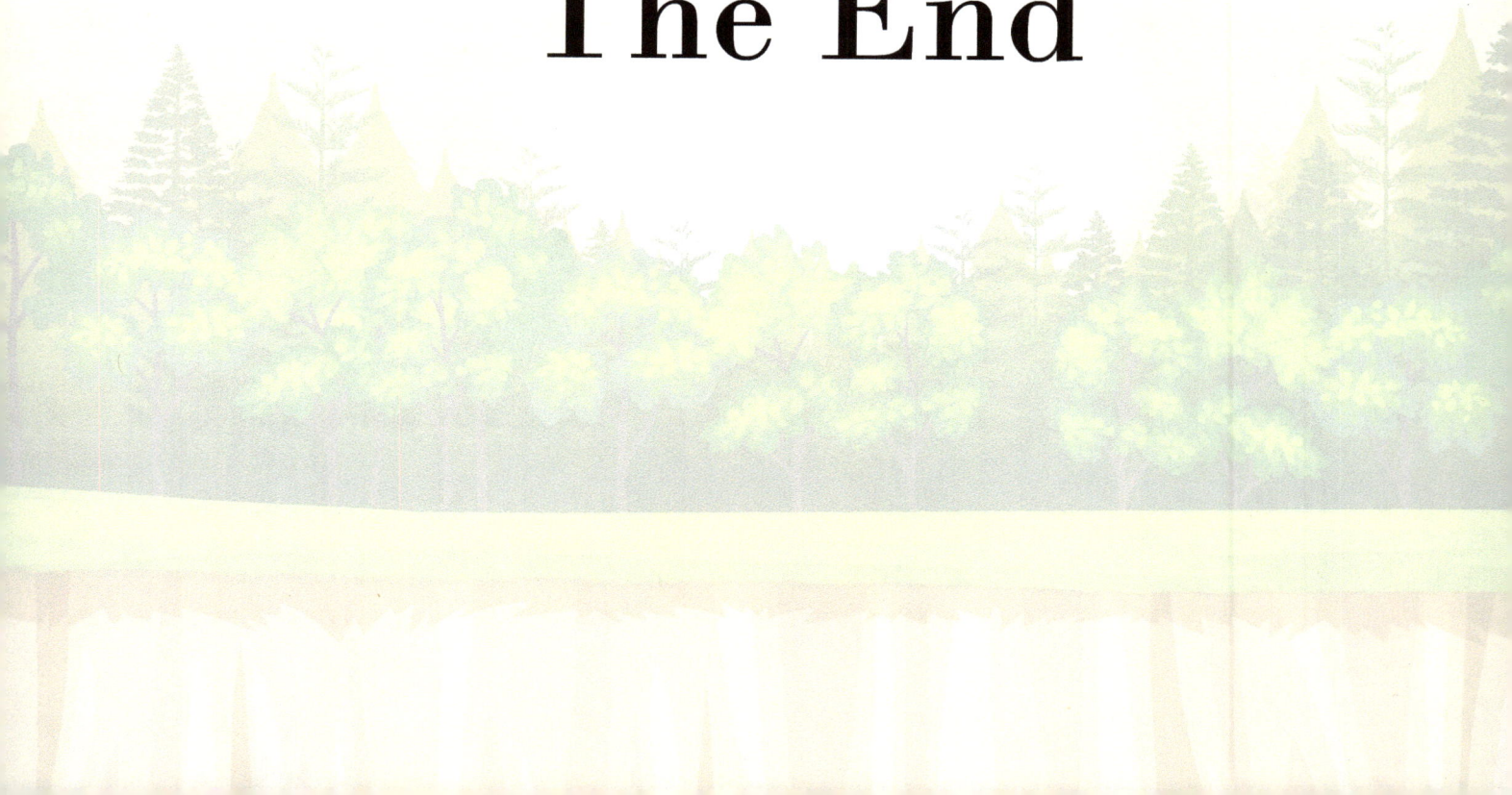

The End

www.ingramcontent.com/pod-product-compliance
Lightning Source LLC
Chambersburg PA
CBHW060813090426

42737CB00002B/50